I0438433

CASTING LIGHT ON DREAMS : A METHOD

© 2012 Sellonge. All rights reserved.
ISBN: 978-1-4716-9450-9

SELLONGE

CASTING LIGHT ON DREAMS : A METHOD

Translation : Deirdre BOLGER

Introduction

According to the point of view presented here, a dream is a rerun of poorly mentalised, subjective psychological experiences that appeared during the day just preceding the dream. Typically, it consists of impressions from the previous day that were experienced in a real, albeit, furtive manner. These impressions are open to introspection but have not reached a "consciousness" level; one could say that they drift in the background.

This approach supports current theories of the waking/dreaming continuity; however, it differs from these in that it focusses on the affective content[1]. For us, a dream appears primarily as a thread of feelings that echo an identical thread of feelings experienced in real-life the day before. The aim of this work is to present the approach that led to these suggestions. We will also present some directions for the continuation of this work.

We limit ourselves to a phenomenological view, thus our approach focusses on representing the observed phenomenon without reference to any explanatory theory and even without raising questions regarding causes or meanings. To this end, we apply a corpus of about fifty dreams; around

---

[1] Affects generally appear as accessories or are regarded as especially liable to be transformed into images, for example when they are difficult to cope with (FREUD). Consequently, such ideas are founded on cognitive paradigms.

forty of these were produced during the phase entailing the validation of the principle of oneiric reruns of poorly mentalised, lived experiences (1997 to beginning of 2002) and about ten of them were produced during the phase of the study of oneiric conversions (the study of the "symbolism") which was started at the beginning of 2012, after an interruption of about ten years.

Fundamental Observations

To approach the study of a dream, we suggest starting by focussing attention on the impressions experienced (sensory-emotional paradigm) rather than on an account of its story (cognitive paradigm) as it seems that the succession of impressions experienced in the dream is a rerun of an identical succession of the same impressions experienced during the preceding day. Thus we examine the dream below (Dream of the killer monster, 971213[2]) in the following manner:

I am in a bedroom. The bed is undone, I am sitting on it. The atmosphere is bleak, there is little light. (Disquiet).

I feel danger, I sense that something bad will befall me. (Anxiety).

I have a pistol (hope), I try it out, I cannot get it to work. It blocks. (Deception).

Then arrives a giant who has come to kill me. (Anxiety).

He approaches, seats himself next to me and grabs me to kill me. (Intense terror).

I try to use the pistol. It's not easy, it is difficult to operate, I have to use my two hands. (Embarrassment).

I manage to fire three shots at his head (success, hope). He shows obvious signs of being hit but this does not prevent

------

[2] 971213: dream from the night of the 12 to 13th December 1997.

7

him from continuing the attack .(Deception accompanied by increased anxiety).

I tell myself that if I shoot him in the private parts he will become my slave. (Hope).

I fire three shots at him in that area without conviction. (Ambivalent hope).

To see if he has really become my slave, I tell him to leave (ambivalent hope). He leaves (satisfaction). I fear that he will not remain my slave (anxiety).

I tell him to go to another person's home (I don't know whose), a person I do not like (hope). I think that, in that way, I will not fall victim to a rebellion (relief, anxiety), I also hope that he will treat that enemy badly. He goes there but does not cause that person too much trouble (deception).

While the approach generally used to access a dream is through its story ("I am in a bedroom. The bed is undone etc...."), here we suggest beginning by, at first, distancing oneself from the story. This allows one to focus on the sequence of affects, in this case: Disquiet / Anxiety / Hope / Deception / Anxiety / Intense terror / Embarrassment / Success, hope / Deception and increased anxiety etc.

It turns out that this series of affects traces an identical series of real-life affective states experienced the previous day, it displays a real similarity with the real-life experiences. In what follows, the relevance of this finding will become apparent

In the present case: the previous day, I read a text on the subject of illusion[3]. Consequently I reflected on the possible tendency "to take flight in dreams", that is the potential tendency to delude myself, to fool myself. This makes me ill at ease. My mood is morose. *I am in a bedroom. The bed is undone, I am sitting on it. The atmosphere is bleak, there is little light (Disquiet).*

The idea that this inclination towards delusion may be excessive or systematic causes me to worry. I sense the risk of disillusionment (""And what if I were to sense that, in this world, the Truth is outside of our reach? It would be catastrophic!"). I have the feeling of being confronted with a serious problem. Anxiety emerges. *I sense danger, I fear that something bad* (grim disillusionment) *will befall me (Anxiety).*

I believe, deep down, that I have the necessary strength of character to defend myself in this type of situation. I have a weapon; a defensive power: "reason", which allows me to return to a "normal" state. Therefore, I feel that I am sufficiently equipped to protect myself. *I have a pistol*[4]; possessing a weapon for self-protection is a source of hope. But my reason allows itself to be dominated by increasing anxiety; it does not manage to establish control. The hope of having a means of defence is dashed. *I test it, I don't manage*

[3] Article, "Lune", J. DES VIGNES ROUGES. Dictionnaire des caractères, Paris, Oliven, 1945.
[4] Knowledge of the real-life story allows the link to be made between the "pistol" / "reason". It is in this way that our method allows us to understand the "symbolism", the characteristics of the dream conversions.

to get it to work. It blocks. The intended weapon, reason, is ineffective *(Deception)*.

This is not an interpretation, it is, rather, a translation: in real-life I felt, at first, capable of defending myself with the aid of reason, but then, faced with one whose strength is greater than mine, I felt inadequate.

Reading the words, "some people suffer life's hurts intensely. Their only remedy to life's ills is to escape into their dreams. This is their morbid, almost desperate means of adapting to life", triggers, in the background, a feeling that could be expressed as: "Were I faced with hurt would I not also simply hid myself through illusion, and, therefore, could I not be, unbeknownst to myself, partly delirious?" Thus, I anticipate a frightening question. My anxiety intensifies. *Then arrives a giant, he is coming to kill me (Anxiety).* This underlying impression (that which could be expressed as, "could I not, unbeknownst to myself, be delirious") is not a hypothesis; it existed in reality and was captured, retrospectively, through introspection. It was drifting furtively in the background.

Continuing to read I am brought back to the memory of a situation in which I was certain of having done something for which I was criticised for not having done, this drags me down further. "But could it be, I start to think, that I had convinced myself of something that was false? In that case, to pursue this line of thought, I must have been fooled by a flawed vision of reality". The idea of having been driven unawares to a distortion of reality and even to seeing the opposite of what I should have seen provokes terror as I now must doubt everything. Truth, even partial truth, does not exist. I view this undetected delirium as having the most catastrophic and insurmountable of consequences. *The monster approaches, sits close to me and grips me to kill me (Intense terror).* This awful terror was, in reality, a fleeting affective gesture (of a brief instant) of poignant intensity[5]. This affect (the experience and the strangeness of it) is such that I am in no doubt as to the parallel between this dream and the reality.

Troubled, I find it hard to reason with myself. I feel that I am trying to struggle against myself, fighting to protect myself. *I try to use the pistol*, namely reason, but to no avail. *It is not easy, it proves difficult to operate, I need to use both of my hands (Embarrassment).*

Etc.

This dream was translated completely and the oneiric rerun of manifest affects experienced in real-life is present throughout and to the end of the dream.

---

[5] The intensity of the terror in the dream was such that I expected to be able to locate within it the terror of the previous day and the incident that gave rise to it. Of all the dreams that I have translated before (about twenty), this particular search proved the longest. The historical source of this terror was difficult to uncover because, although intense, it lasted for a very brief instant.

UNDERLYING AFFECTS AND SENSATIONS

An undercurrent of affective and emotional content overlays the manifest affects. Thus, the following (Godille while skiing, February 1997):

Dream	Manifest Affects	Experiences of the previous day
I am with someone and I am skiing.	Pleasure Slight fear of falling.	My theoretical research is accompanied by an impression that could be described as "*everything seems to very clear*", hence the feeling of pleasure. However, there is a slight anxiousness, the fear that difficulties may arise.

Dream	Manifest Affects	Experiences of the previous day
I stop and an anonymous skier almost knocks me down.	Feeling of instability Fear	Objections appear, they become more and more serious (a source of real feelings of instability). One of these relates to a refutation, its seriousness is such that the ensuing impression could be expressed as, *"and what if I am mistaken in everything?"* (Fear).
My colleague tells me that it is my fault; the anonymous skier gestures in support of this.	Guilt	I feel that I am to blame for this situation (guilt).

These events are accompanied by "underlying" impressions that echo, also, real-life experiences from the previous day.

Thus, in our extract:

Dream	Underlying Impressions	Real-life experiences of the previous day
I am with someone and I am skiing.	I feel myself being as being accompanied. I have the sensation of skiing.	I feel the support of an "Alter Ego" who imbues me with insight. I have the feeling of moving forward with ease (gliding sensation).
I stop and the anonymous skier almost knocks me down.	The feeling of moving forward transforms into a feeling of being stationary. A risk of being knocked down.	Because of the objection, to which I can find no response, I feel that I have come to a stand-still in the advancement of the theory. I fear that the disillusionment felt at not being able to counter the objection will bring me down.

Dream	Underlying Impressions	Real-life experiences of the previous day
My colleague tells me that it is my fault; the anonymous skier gestures in support of this.	I feel that the person accompanying me is placing the blame on me. Moderate guilt.	I feel self-criticism coming from a source other than "Me". The self-criticism is not insistent.

THE GENERALITY OF THE PHENOMENON

Over a period of five years (1997 to 2001) it was possible to build up a corpus of 43 dreams of which one was lucid (and creative). Gradually, as the translations proceeded, the idea of a general principle of the oneiric rerun of impressions from real-life experiences of the previous day became increasingly incontrovertible. This was verified by a general and quantified synthesis of the data of the entire sample group (All the dreams recorded during this period were included; there was no selection). Of the 43 dreams studies, 14 of them displayed echoes that were so convincing that the correspondence between the dreamed and real-life impressions was beyond doubt[6].

---

[6] Indisputable echoes occurred in the case of a recurrence of intense

The issue, therefore, became one of determining if this rerun only applies to certain impressions in a dream or if all the impressions in a dream have been experienced already in real-life during the previous day. The study of all the identified dreamed impressions confirmed this phenomenon of echoing for 91% of the 516 manifest affects gathered; this result takes into account the constraint of temporal homogeneity[7].

Such echoing also appears to relate to the underlying oneiric affects. This level of insight facilitates a more detailed and a deeper analysis. Unfortunately, for technical reasons, this study could not be carried out exhaustively. However, although it was not possible to be exhaustive in our study, it was possible to be global. In the present case, if, in the context of a scene-by-scene study, the underlying oneiric impressions identified "on the fly" corresponded to real impressions experienced, the dreamed scene was considered compatible with the real-life incident. Such compatibility appeared in 70% of the 344 scenes recorded. Rather than proving that the dream was independent of the real-life experience of the previous day, the remaining 30% could be considered as resulting from a lack of expertise and/or as relating to memories.

---

affective impressions, as in the case of the terror and despair accompanying situations of near-death, of intense wonder...but also in the case of sensations such as the that of adrenaline pumping, where the effect of emotions is felt in the flesh (blows, shocks, pleasure,...). These echoes also appear in the case of milder and, in particular, less common impressions (feelings that are a mixture of the sensation of one's stomach contracting and that of being absorbed, the very unusual sensation of being scrubbed and scoured in the shower...)

[7] Not only are the manifest affects identical to the affects of the previous day, but they also present the same story and the same order occurrence.

As temporal order was respected (not only was there a reappearance of impressions, but also the succession of dreamed impressions traced exactly the succession of real-life impressions) it is interesting to examine how the real-life scenes follow each other within a single point in time. In this case, we can speculate on the possibility of either a restitution of homogenous processes or an arbitrary restitution of unrelated scenes scattered throughout the day.

A study of the temporal distribution of the real-life sequence of events that sparked the dream revealed that, in 74% of cases, it was certain that the dreams reproduced a single moment of a person's life from the previous day. There were doubts, but no strong contradictory evidence, regarding this in the case of the remaining dreams (Note that the principle of a rerun of impressions also "operates" in real life[8]. This rerun of impressions could, therefore, be a source of confusion between the events and one's memories of the events thus giving rise to an amalgam of both. In this case, despite being scattered across time, the story in question still remains homogenous).

In all we estimated that:

---

[8] We could be reminded of Proust's madeleines in which the reproduction of impressions reaches conscious awareness. Experienced during the initial scene, such impressions can reappear in an allusive manner when one is recalling certain events and, thus, it is sometimes difficult to ascertain if a dreamed impression relates to its initial context as it occurred that day, or from its evocation later in the day. We are also reminded of unpleasant flashbacks, which carry with them intense affects experienced during traumatic events.

43% of dreams provide strong evidence in favour of the principle of oneiric rerun of impressions experienced during the previous day (100% correspondence between manifest affects and genuine real-life impressions experienced the previous day, and at least 80% of scenes judged as being "compatible" on the basis of underlying oneiric affects).

28% of dreams are compatible with this principle (at least 90% correspondence between manifest affects and genuine real-life impressions experienced the previous day, and at least 50%, or even 80% in the case of short dreams, of scenes judged "compatible" on the basis of underlying oneiric affects).

The other dreams are debatable due only to, more or less, partial vagueness or gaps in the memories. The lucid dream conforms to our principle (the impression of being in control of the dream that appeared to be echoing the impression experienced the previous day, of conducting a process with a view to gaining an understanding).

Comments on the methodology

Of course, we need to acknowledge the scientific limits of a subjective comparison of affective states. We refer, on the one hand, to the often criticised method of introspection and, on the other hand, we refer to the subjective method of the comparison of affective states.

But, is it possible to judge if a deception experienced in a dream corresponds to a particular deception experienced in real-life? For the moment, we can only satisfy ourselves with our subjective method while looking forward to the advent of a metrological means of capturing the relevant cerebral activity. Although this subjective method falls short of the possible contributions of future technological means, it can be justified if one bears in mind that "the impression of being" that everyone experiences in their dreams through the intermediary of a central character and "the impression of being" experienced in real-life are judged as similar to such an extent that one has no doubt but that the central character in the dream, although generally invisible, is him or herself. This echoing, experienced by everyone, legitimises an approach based on a matching with real-life feelings. But even if this method does have flaws, it still possesses one decisive advantage: that of grounding the study on facts.

Concerning introspection, we do not define it as the examination of the "consciousness" by itself because we regard "consciousness" as a highly mentalised product of introspection. As we see a dream as a rerun of poorly mentalised feelings, the result of unintentional perceiving, we suggest concentrating on the "perceptual act", a "perceptual activity" that is more or less intentional and mentalizing and operating in the "psychic" environment. It is this "perceptual act" that we refer to as "introspection" and we say that this introspection converts a psychic state into a psychological experience, with experience being described as "consciousness" in the specific case of a sufficiently mentalised percept. Another kind of conversion could also be at work here: the mentalised elements, representative and/or affective, are also transformed into words with the result that the psychological experience can be converted into a psychological concept. Hence, an introspective psychology is developed, which is based on intentional (and verbalised) introspection. We do not claim that this solution is perfect, but we do assert its potential[9]. We do not wish to reduce psychology to an introspective psychology. Rather, we suggest that there is scope for introspection and it is this that we wish to study.

---

[9] DIEL showed how intentional introspection can be methodical.

For our part, in addition to questions regarding verbalisation we have also been confronted with the following questions in our study:

The distorting effect of vanity, that inclination which leads one to forge an image that satisfies the Ego (DIEL).

Avoidance out of fear. Not knowing what may surface from their introspections and, fearing the worse, the person becomes frightened. They have the feeling of being overwhelmed, but have no knowledge of the enemy against which they will have to struggle. So that they fear the dominating force of this enemy and feel insufficiently equipped to defend themselves against an anxiety, the devastating effect of which they dread, against a feeling of guilt or remorse which carries the fear of agonising torment...The dread of a confrontation causes them to flee or to become paralysed (and all the more so in the case of excessive vanity).

We are not, however, completely without the means of responding to these two biases. These biases may arise but this does not always occur and even when they do appear, their impact is not sufficiently strong to disturb to any large extent a methodological bringing to consciousness. Distortion through vanity, like taking flight out of fear, can give rise to psychological experiences that facilitate the detection and, thus, the correction of these biases. Time also has a part to play in that it mellows the passions; thus one way of reducing the bias is to defer the refinement of a translation until a later time.

It may also be helpful to remember that the shortcomings related to observation (and/or its transcription) is a phenomenon common to all sciences, that an improvement in observation occurs when a theory can suggest where and how to look and that improvements in observation bring about new theoretical developments. Why would this be different for psychology? Introspection should progress in parallel with developments in the psychology of introspection.

Beyond these general considerations, our method relies upon the technical quality of the observations: a written record of a dream can vary in its detail and accuracy and a translation, that is, the linking of a poorly mentalised, psychological experience, depends on the quality of recollecting.

The technique of translation

The translation technique suggested here is based on the principle of an echoing between the dreamed impressions and the poorly mentalised, real-life psychological experiences of the previous day. This relationship allows us to examine on beneficial "equation".

The image in the dream (which is known) associated with an impression experienced in the dream (which is also known)

=

The poorly mentalised impression from the previous day (recognisable as it relates to the impression experienced in the dream) associated with a trigger (to be uncovered).

Using this "equation" it is possible to make a link between the triggering event from one's life during previous day and the oneiric image. The translation begins, therefore, in a concrete manner by searching for the real-life impressions that were experienced the day before the dream and played out again in the dream. Having found these impressions, the dream can be linked to a particular experience from the previous day.

To facilitate the translation, and to enable the recollection of the past experience, I generally transcribe the dream into a table with three-columns. I begin by writing, in sentence-form, the story of the dream in the left-hand column. Then, I focus on the manifest affective states experienced in the dream; these I transcribe into the central column. Once this task has been completed, I tackle the "the recollection of feelings of the previous day" part, which involves recalling the events themselves and the experiences. This is time-consuming and one should reserve a morning to search for the triggering event of the dream and an afternoon for the completion of a reasonable recapitulation of the stages in the story. Difficulties may arise from the fact that the impressions experienced in real-life are poorly mentalised experiences, background fluctuations, underlying ideo-affective shiftings[10]. These fluctuations and states are more felt than formalised and, although open to introspection, they drift, unbeknownst to ourselves, in parallel to "conscious" thoughts and perceptions. They present a particular case.

---

[10] If the words "profession" or "love life"... are uttered during the course of a discussion, certain interlocutors may suffer a dim episode or flashes of intense euphoria, of anxiety, of regret...depending on their past and their sensitivities. But if one's attention remains captured by the exchange of ideas taking place, it may not latch onto these echos which could have, in a certain manner, contributed to the person's experience without fully revealing itself. The phenomenon remains as an undercurrent, poorly mentalised. Conversely, it could be that these ideo-affective shifts recapture one's attention which is then diverted from the conversation. The affective component is, therefore, manifested as outward emotions and/or the idealistic component (formerly a simple, allusive synthesis of a past and/or a future in ones professional life, love-life etc.) is brought to "consciousness" as representations occupying one's mind completely. To summarize therefore, neglected by an attention that is diverted essentially by phenomena with greater powers of attraction, the ideo-affective reactions to percepts (words, images, odors, sounds,...) drift in the background; hence the formation of an underlying ideo-affective life.

Thus, for example, we present the following extract (A dream about an underground septic tank, February 1997):

I am in front of the family home and I am being shown a crack in the exterior wall, at the back of the house, next to the living room (Disquiet). I feel embarrassed because I do not know how to repair it. (Embarrassment)

It is then that my father shows me something that worries me even more: an enormous gaping vertical crack. (Increased embarrassment)

Looking closely at it, it seems that one entire part of the building has split in two horizontally: its upper part having become detached from the lower part and separated by a gap. (Catastrophe and resignation)

I am angry with myself for not having noticed this myself earlier, being, as I was, responsible for the upkeep of the house. (Shame, guilt)

Etc.

1) I write it down in the following manner:

Stages of the dream	Manifest affects	Translation
I am in front of the family home and I am being shown a crack in the exterior wall, at the back of the house, close to the living-room.	Disquiet	
I feel embarrassed because I do not know how to repair it.	Embarras-sment	
It is then that my father shows me something that worries me more: a large, gaping, vertical crack.	Increased embarras-sment	
Looking closely at it, it seems that one entire part of the building has split in two horizontally: its upper part having become detached from the lower part and separated by a gap.	Catastro-phe and resigna-tion	
I am angry with myself for not having noticed this earlier, being, as I was, responsible for the upkeep of the house.	Shame and guilt	

2) I search for the moment during the previous day in which I experienced the succession of, Disquiet/ Embarrassment / Increased embarrassment / Catastrophe and resignation / Shame, guilt etc. In practice, I begin by concentrating on the general atmosphere of the dream (turbulent, peaceful, morbid, euphoric, superiority / inferiority, anxiety, enthusiasm,...) and I compare it to the different "interior" states of the previous day (I gather recollections of the day beginning with daybreak). If possible, I uncover the theme repeated by the dream, a theme that may have appeared several times during the day. Thus, I compare the dreamed affects with the real-life experiences that appeared at these different times of the day until I find an overlap of dreamed/lived affects for a particular moment. It is also possible to work from the basis of a particularly striking affect or sensation. But, a strong emotion could prove difficult to uncover because if it is morbid it will last for only a very fleeting instant.

In the case of our example:

Stages of the dream	Manifest affects	Translation
I am in front of the family home and I am being shown a crack in the exterior wall, at the back of the house, close to the living-room.	Disquiet	I am working on a dream with scenes considered despicable.

Of course, and here lies a difficulty, the manifest oneiric affect, in this case *"disquiet"*, is a rerun of the disquiet experienced in real-life during the previous day, a disquiet that is, however, poorly mentalised. This is not the real, mentalised affect, shame in this case (presented with these despicable scenes I am moved to shame), rather it is something that drifts in the background. Behind the shame, the primary experience, a feeling of anxiety had unfolded at a secondary level. But this anxiety had not yet reached consciousness.

Stages of the dream	Manifest affects	Translation
I feel embarrassed because I do not know how to repair it.	Embarrassment	I spot one impression that could be expressed by *"Hold on, it appears that I possess that shameful desire"* (embarrassment)

It is then that my father shows me something that worries me more: a large, gaping, vertical crack.	Increased embarrassment	Then an impression that could be expressed as: *"But it seems that I must be contemptible as it appears that I want this desire to be fulfilled"* (increase of embarrassment)
Looking closely at it, it seems that one entire part of the building has split in two horizontally: its upper part having become detached from the lower part and separated by a gap.	Catastrophe and resignation	Then, an impression of the type: *" How dreadful I am"* (panic an resignation).
I am angry with myself for not having noticed this myself earlier, being, as I was, responsible for the upkeep of the house.	Shame, guilt	And finally, *"You are a disgrace"* (shame, guilt)

3) Entering the intrapsychic level

In the example presented here, the translation would have been insufficient if it had ended at this level because another story was being played out in parallel: I was not only dealing with a disturbing feeling for having judged myself disgraceful because of feeling certain desires, I was dealing with a disturbing feeling for not being able to confront this. Thus, the presence of two parallel stories: one concerning an increasingly strong self-perceived indignity (a growing disturbance caused by the perception of being the carrier of shameful desires), and one concerning the emerging of a psychological reaction emerging at a different level, a level that we refer to as "intrapsychic". In the present case, the oneiric impressions were provoked by a pessimistic response to an underlying question at an intrapsychic level, genuinely experienced but in a less evident manner, a question that could be expressed as: "will I manage to deal with this "interior" problem and, thus, make peace with myself?". Thus, a more complete translation would give the following:

Stages of the dream	1st degree translation	2nd degree translation
I am in front of the family home and I am being shown a crack in the exterior wall, at the back of the house, close to the living-room.	I am working on a dream with scenes considered shameful.	My Ego, the image that I have of myself, (the house viewed from outside) is no longer felt with in the usual stable manner.
I feel embarrassed because I do not know how to repair it.	I spot one impression that could be expressed by "*Hold on, it appears that I possess that shameful desire*" (embarrassment)	I have premonitions of a break-down (the house is showing cracks) and I am not sure that I will manage to recover (embarrassment).
It is then that my father shows me something that worries me more: a large, gaping, vertical crack.	Then an impression that could be expressed as: "*But it seems that I must be contemptible as it appears that I want this desire to be fulfilled*" (increase of	I have an insight , a real-life experience from the previous day that seems to originate from a force at work

	embarrassment)	that is outside Me[11], an intuition, accurate or false which could be expressed as follows: "*See the danger that your Ego is in, it is more serious than you first thought* (the crack is enormous). *It will not be easy for you to regain a positive self-esteem*" (Increased embarrassment).
Looking closely at it, it seems that one entire part of the building has split in two horizontally: its upper part having become detached from the	Then an impression of the type: "*How dreadful I am*" (panic an resignation).	Underneath, I panic; I feel myself losing my rational means of control: I feel myself losing my sense of judgement, I feel

---

[11] Here is an Alter Ego: the father as a result of a certain form of (self)-authority.

lower part and separated by a gap.		overwhelmed. The state experienced could be expressed as: *"But, what is happening to me? What is happening? What will become of me?"* (Panic, resignation).
I am angry with myself for not having noticed this myself earlier, being, as I was, responsible for the upkeep of the house.	And finally, *"You are a disgrace"* (shame, guilt)	In addition to these devastating disturbances there is the feeling of guilt and shame towards myself. I criticize myself, me who is striving to know myself and to foster a capacity to confront psychologically my failure (Shame, guilt).

In this extract, I was confronting bad thoughts; these were revisited in the 1st degree translation. But these thoughts were becoming traumatic as I did not consider myself capable of dealing with their traumatising effect; this is the scenario in the 2nd degree translation[12].

In our case, we carry out the task of recalling the day following the dream, lying down, eyes closed and in silent surroundings. A morning is required to identify the real-life moment picked up on in the dream; an afternoon is needed to complete a first linking of the entire dream with reality. This technique, therefore, imposes one very important practical

---

[12] One means to avoid being too affected by arousing thoughts is to act on the thoughts in question. This is, typically, a matter of justifying, of a readjustment of ideas, of *"repressing"*... The objective here is to promote and conserve the "good" thoughts and to destroy, avoid or distance the "bad". The dynamism that causes one to intervene through the use of stimulants (typically through the production and/or taking of positive stimulants; by the destruction and/or avoidance of negative stimulants, including the situation where the stimulants in question are thoughts) is an extroverted dynamism.

But another way of not being affected by a stimulant is to intervene at the level of sensitivity. This consists in moderating one's susceptibility (decrease the objective, relativise one's affects so that the urge becomes less important). The dynamism that consists in intervening through expectancies is an introverted dynamism. It manifests itself in dreams in the form of scenarios that take place indoors (in a room, in a basement,...).

In introverted dreams (those taking place indoors) access to the intrapsychic level is fairly direct. It is less so in extroverted dreams where there appears to be a parallel between the psychic and intrapsychic impressions. A feeling of anxiety, for example, could lead to a feeling of anxiousness at not being able to cope with the anxiety. The dream replays the story of this "mounting anxiousness", a story that could not be reconsidered if we satisfy ourselves with only a 1st degree translation.

condition: the day following the dream must be entirely free of other commitments.

Dreams with original impressions, especially in regard to the general atmosphere or dreams with particularly strong emotions or sensations (fall, pain, pleasure,...) constitute materials of the utmost importance; the discovery of a link between them and a real-life experience appears particularly compelling. One has the benefit, therefore, of excellent materials with which to study the oneiric conversions (the "symbols").

On the other hand, the translation of dreams with banal impressions is open to question because, unless it is long, we can always doubt if it is indeed related to an identified real-life experience and not to another that we simply did not manage to recall.

Evaluation and perspectives

Scientism characterises the "scientific" quality of a representation. "Scientific" can be placed opposition to "ideologic" when the scientific approach consists in basing a theory on facts (the theory is, therefore, the variable to be adjusted) and not in partially using descriptions of facts to support a theory (in this case the variable to be adjusted is the transcription of the facts; therefore selections, generalisations, extrapolations, concealment or even inventions are employed according to ideological requirements).

According to one approach, science is, by nature, subjective (psycho-centred) as all representation is viewed as depending on the senses (even when their influence is rendered less direct through the use of instruments) and the human mind. But this subjectivity, far from being uncontrollable and capricious, can be reasonably impartial, pragmatically realistic; in a word, scientific[13].

---

[13] H. POINCARÉ reminds us that time, for example, although the essence of subjectivity (because it is humankind that judges a particular phenomenon as periodic and of having constant period) can, using a certain formula, be objectified (judging that such a phenomenon is periodic, humankind takes a reference point and, thus, creates a standard). Once the rule has been defined and followed, the measurement of time becomes independent of intentionality which brings time into the realm of science. But, POINCARÉ reminds us, extra-terrestrials with more refined senses than ours may perceive a temporal irregularity where we would see a periodic regularity.

If knowledge can be built scientifically and developed impartially, it can also be transformed by emotions or partiality for ideological reasons or through the simple effect of enchantment (such as the lucidity of love). It is for this reason that scientific perception should begin by clearing the object of the study of all emotional content.

Let us imagine, as an illustration, the state of mind of our ancestors as they stand before a tree-god (before an intentioned-tree). No doubt they were the puppets of their own fears and their hopes, and the weight of these emotions would have made them view the tree in a manner very much removed from ours[14].

But, from this point of view, what is the status of the dream? Indeed, today we can question the scientific status of the dream as, very often, we consider it as having an aura of magic. This troubles those who, for example, see the dream as a bearer of messages from the Depths or from All-Knowing powers above. Conversely others, as if by a kind of heretical ambivalence, consider the dream as nothing more than an incoherent residue of cerebral functioning. Thus, it would appear that the aim of clearing this object of emotion has yet to be accomplished.

---

[14] We might like to imagine certain optimists by nature who, in addition, have been calmed by certain protective rites; they find themselves, therefore, less emotive in the presence of the "tree-god-from-which-I-am-protected" and begin to view it differently, to inspect it in a manner that is more rational, more "scientific".

For us, the dream appears to repeat a lived experience from the previous day with the sagacity of a parrot. Like a parrot, which repeats that which it has heard exactly as it heard it, a dream echoes judgements from the previous day in their original form, be them accurate or false, relevant or outrageous etc. The dream acts as neither a critic nor a commentator.

Just like a parrot, which does not select what it says based on its importance, a dream appears to provide a rerun of incidental events, that can often be even trivial, not crucial moments in one's life by virtue of a message, a warning, a general appraisal or other highly valuable indicators that a phase of one's life may carry.

To summarise therefore, just as in the case of the parrot from which we expect neither a revelation nor a judgement, a dream should not be viewed as an important carrier of meanings, considered thus it could generate anxiety and thus become pathogenic.

A dream, we note, is a representation of a poorly mentalised, real-life psychological experience, a representation with a structure that is in sync with the historical sources[15]. If, in practice, the building of this representation is based on defined conversions (this idea remains, for the moment, a line of exploration) then the dream comes to resemble a sensor with which "psychological things" from one's life during the previous day are converted into "oneiric stuff"[16], and including

---

[15] We sense, in the translations, a certain logic in the setting down of the images and attributes.

[16] As we saw with the example of the killer monster, the linking of the

a transposition of a hierarchical structure from the psychological domain. Indeed the conversion appears measured (a matter here of suggestions inferred from observations). There is nothing, therefore, to stop one from being opportunist and basing a psychology on elementary concepts that could correspond to the "psychological things" experienced the previous day that were converted into "oneiric stuff" according to a constant conversion (that is to say, bijective and transposable to all).

In light of this, the development of a psychology could be based on discovering certain fundamentals of a dream (a fundamental is "oneiric stuff" that seems to be linked systematically to the same "psychological thing" experienced the day before) and on the understanding of the "psychological things" that these fundamentals may represent. These "psychological things" would, therefore, constitute elementary concepts. The traditional, "what does this image mean?" would thus become: "such an image, what does it define, or what does it measure?".

On basing ourselves on the equation of translation, we enter our approach on the dreamed element that provides the framework for the story of the dream. We question ourselves, in concrete terms, regarding the reality relating to the fact that the story of the dream takes place indoors (there is, therefore, an underlying impression of confinement) rather than outside (where there is an underlying feeling of being able to extend

---

dreamed story and the real-life story allows us to view the pistol "oneiric stuff" as an oneiric conversion of "reason" ("psychological thing").

ourselves). Believing in a hypothesised legal exposure (that is, based on the idea that differentiating between scenes taking place indoor and scenes taking place outside always indicates a difference in the type of experience), we compared the poorly mentalised, real-life experiences at the origin of the interior dreams to those at the origin of the exterior dreams in the hope of finding, among the experiences of the previous day, something that differentiates them. We feel that we have achieved this and have found two complementary dynamics which, invariably, were converted, one into interior scenes, the other into exterior scenes.

An analogous situation arose while we were trying to locate what was exposing "the human actor in the dream", or even "the central hero of the dream". In the two cases, we believe that we have located the psychological objects that were transformed into human-beings by the instigator of the dreams.

There is nothing, therefore, to prevent us from deciding upon a terminology that relates directly to this conversion. For example, "introversion (...extraversion) is the psychological thing that is converted in the indoor scenes (...outside)". It is in this way that acquiring sufficient experience in translating dreams will allow us to "see" that which JUNG had such difficulty in explaining. Hence, if consistent conversions exist (that is, valid for all) their identification help us develop a clear and precise terminology that is concrete and that acts as an indisputable reference point, since its concepts would be based on a procedure that facilitates the convergence of the introspective view and the psychological element in question.

The study of oneiric conversions, through the rigourous application of a concrete equation, can provide a means of achieving a satisfactory terminology. And in addition, in acting as "movies" of a poorly mentalised, psychological process and in not being modified by any intentional bringing to consciousness, the dream and its translation may, therefore, also become the basic materials for a study of psychological functioning.

Studying dreams

The advancement of our understanding of dreams is based firstly on translation. This can be distinguished from interpretation in that the latter is an extrapolation founded on analogies while a translation is a conversion of an oneiric expression (the dream) into an expression of past events.

Thus, for example, the interpreter, making the link between how they conduct themselves real-life and driving themselves in a car may do so based on an a priori theoretical conception. This conception could, for example, define one's personality based on the polarities of masculine and feminine and thus lead the interpreter to transform "*I am a passenger in a car driven by a woman*" into "you allow your feminine side to control your life". In the case of the translator, basing his or herself on the similarity between experiences, they will view the lady-driver as a specific Alter Ego (for example, the social side of the dreamer, or maybe their devious, worldly, artistic, etc. sides) and the car as a particular subject on which he or she is working (a particular matter, a certain project, a particular aspect of one's life,...). They might say, for example, "yesterday, during a professional matter with which I was preoccupied, I allowed myself to be lead by my intuition which awakened my devious side, a side which, rightly or wrongly, enchanted me on this occasion[17]".

---

[17] In the case of a man.

This example provides us with an opportunity to present certain novel principles which now appear to be taking shape:

-   Understanding is based on the perspective of one's particular position. While dreams are generally regarded as expressing the fundamental and constant elements of the dreamer's personality, we believe that dreams can reveal completely singular aspects that emerged in a specific context; in our example, we would have been wrong to conclude that the "the dreamer is a devious person". Without trying to presuppose what their normal behaviour might be, a more accurate translation would be "in the real-life moment replayed by the dream, the dreamer acted in a devious manner". The translation is situated.

-   Understanding is based on the perspective of an echoing; the dream presents itself as a rerun of the psychology of a past experience and not as a continuation of this experience (fulfilment of a desire, "unconscious" analysis and judgement of all its implications,...). The judgements are those of the dreamer in context and are not extra-consciousness. In the present case, the dreamer feels gripped by an inclination to be devious, an inclination that appears to carry a certain amount of attractiveness (this could be used to point out the difference between a man/man relationship and a man/woman relationship). We do not consider this as a manifestation of extra-consciousness, which presumes that the dreamer was not in control of his or her own actions[18].

- The apprehension is personal. The dreamer is the only person who can translate his or her dream since they alone have intimate knowledge of their past. An experienced translator (of their own dreams) can suggest possible ways of deciphering in the case of the dreams already encountered, the events of which they translated. But this is only an aid to the translation.

The study of dreams also consists in the observation of the inherent elements of dreams. Thus, for example, given a dream about divers swimming amidst "under-water stuff" in which it is not known whether the "stuff" is living (vegetal) or inert (rock), we need to make the following inference: although there is a difference between the living and the inert, there also exists a common genetic basis between the two and,

---

[18] This comment poses the question of the use of dreams in a psychoanalytic setting. An essentialist psychoanalytical apprehension resulting from a conception that is based on an extra-conscious compass (the interpretation of a dream allows one to identify any deviations from an "unconscious" Meaning, deviations that are a source of psychic disturbances) is replaced, here, by an existentialist apprehension in which the person his or herself develops his or her Meaning. This engages "social facts", that is, they interact with *"ways of behaving, of thinking and of feeling that are external to individual and which are endowed with the coercive power to impose themselves on him "* (DURKHEIM), elements that have been interiorised since childhood and are susceptible to collective development. To avoid the psycho-analyst becoming the director of the consciousness, we tend to suggest a Kantian approach. In the present case, to encourage the development of Meaning, without imposing their own, one could ask the question: "what would happen if everyone systematically chose deviousness?". Note also that the dream, even untranslated, remains a means of entering another person's Universe because "it gives voice to" and reveal aspects of the person.

thus, we would be wrong to suggest a symbolism denying such common-ground between the "living" and the "inert". Similarly, it can be said that an animal in a dream and a character in a dream share common genetic characteristics since I dreamt of a woman who was transformed into a dog and who was then transformed back into a woman[19]. In the event of encountering a dream in which there is a vegetable/animal transformation we should conclude the existence of a common substrate of all the visual elements of the dream.

---

[19] The woman was transformed into a rothweller and then regained her original form. On an internet forum, a woman described a similar dream in which, "as if by magic", a man was temporarily transformed in a dog "like a rothweller".

Conclusion

A dream involves a rerun of a poorly mentalised, real-life psychological experience that occurred only a short time before it was produced. Therefore, it presents itself as neither an incoherent residue of cerebral functioning nor as an important carrier of a message that was created extra-consciously.

The interpretation of dream, a decoding activity that is rooted in an a priori explanatory framework, does not appear legitimate to us. We suggest adopting the role of a translator who, starting with the oneiric reruns, works towards the real-life psychological experiences and, from them, infers the explanatory framework. Therefore, it is not so much the psychology that brings one to an understanding of dreams but the understanding of dreams that leads to the development of the psychology.

CONTENTS

Introduction 5

Fundamental Observations 7

   RERUN OF MANIFEST AFFECTS 7

   UNDERLYING AFFECTS AND SENSATIONS 12

   THE GENERALITY OF THE PHENOMENON 15

Comments on the methodology 19

The technique of translation 23

Evaluation and perspectives 36

Studying dreams 42

Conclusion 46

BIBLIOGRAPHY

DIEL P., Psychologie de la motivation, Paris, Petite Bibliothèque Payot, 1969.

DURKHEIM E., Les règles de la méthode sociologique, Paris, Flammarion, 2010.

FREUD S., Sur les rêves, Paris, Gallimard, 1988.

JUNG C.G., Types psychologiques, Genève, Georg, 1954.

KANT E., Fondements de la métaphysique des mœurs, Paris, Le Livre de Poche, 1993.

POINCARÉ, H., La science et l'hypothèse, Paris, Flammarion, 2009.

www.ingramcontent.com/pod-product-compliance
Lightning Source LLC
Chambersburg PA
CBHW031333290526
45784CB00014B/2648